VEHICLE MAINTENANCE LOG BOOK

This log book belongs to:

_____

_____

_____

VEHICLE DETAILS

_____

_____

License Plate No: _____ **VEHICLE MAINTENANCE LOG BOOK** **Make/Model/Year:** _____

DATE	DESCRIPTION OF WORK DONE	MILEAGE	LOCATION/ COMPANY	REPLACEMENT PARTS (if applicable)	COST

License Plate No: _____   **VEHICLE MAINTENANCE LOG BOOK**   **Make/Model/Year:** _____

DATE	DESCRIPTION OF WORK DONE	MILEAGE	LOCATION/ COMPANY	REPLACEMENT PARTS *(if applicable)*	COST

License Plate No: _____ **VEHICLE MAINTENANCE LOG BOOK** **Make/Model/Year:** _____

DATE	DESCRIPTION OF WORK DONE	MILEAGE	LOCATION/ COMPANY	REPLACEMENT PARTS (if applicable)	COST

License Plate No: _____ **VEHICLE MAINTENANCE LOG BOOK** **Make/Model/Year:** _____

DATE	DESCRIPTION OF WORK DONE	MILEAGE	LOCATION/ COMPANY	REPLACEMENT PARTS *(if applicable)*	COST

License Plate No: _____   **VEHICLE MAINTENANCE LOG BOOK**   **Make/Model/Year:** _____

DATE	DESCRIPTION OF WORK DONE	MILEAGE	LOCATION/ COMPANY	REPLACEMENT PARTS (if applicable)	COST

License Plate No: _____   **VEHICLE MAINTENANCE LOG BOOK**   **Make/Model/Year:** _____

DATE	DESCRIPTION OF WORK DONE	MILEAGE	LOCATION/ COMPANY	REPLACEMENT PARTS (if applicable)	COST

License Plate No: _____   **VEHICLE MAINTENANCE LOG BOOK**   **Make/Model/Year:** _____

DATE	DESCRIPTION OF WORK DONE	MILEAGE	LOCATION/ COMPANY	REPLACEMENT PARTS *(if applicable)*	COST

License Plate No: _____   **VEHICLE MAINTENANCE LOG BOOK**   **Make/Model/Year:** _____

DATE	DESCRIPTION OF WORK DONE	MILEAGE	LOCATION/ COMPANY	REPLACEMENT PARTS (if applicable)	COST

License Plate No: _____   **VEHICLE MAINTENANCE LOG BOOK**   **Make/Model/Year:** _____

DATE	DESCRIPTION OF WORK DONE	MILEAGE	LOCATION/ COMPANY	REPLACEMENT PARTS (if applicable)	COST

License Plate No: _____ **VEHICLE MAINTENANCE LOG BOOK** **Make/Model/Year:** _____

DATE	DESCRIPTION OF WORK DONE	MILEAGE	LOCATION/ COMPANY	REPLACEMENT PARTS *(if applicable)*	COST

License Plate No: _____   **VEHICLE MAINTENANCE LOG BOOK**   Make/Model/Year: _____

DATE	DESCRIPTION OF WORK DONE	MILEAGE	LOCATION/ COMPANY	REPLACEMENT PARTS *(if applicable)*	COST

License Plate No: _____ **VEHICLE MAINTENANCE LOG BOOK** Make/Model/Year: _____

DATE	DESCRIPTION OF WORK DONE	MILEAGE	LOCATION/ COMPANY	REPLACEMENT PARTS (if applicable)	COST

License Plate No: _____ **VEHICLE MAINTENANCE LOG BOOK** Make/Model/Year: _____

DATE	DESCRIPTION OF WORK DONE	MILEAGE	LOCATION/ COMPANY	REPLACEMENT PARTS (if applicable)	COST

License Plate No: _____   **VEHICLE MAINTENANCE LOG BOOK**   Make/Model/Year: _____

DATE	DESCRIPTION OF WORK DONE	MILEAGE	LOCATION/ COMPANY	REPLACEMENT PARTS *(if applicable)*	COST

License Plate No: _____   **VEHICLE MAINTENANCE LOG BOOK**   Make/Model/Year: _____

DATE	DESCRIPTION OF WORK DONE	MILEAGE	LOCATION/ COMPANY	REPLACEMENT PARTS *(if applicable)*	COST

License Plate No: _____   **VEHICLE MAINTENANCE LOG BOOK**   **Make/Model/Year:** _____

DATE	DESCRIPTION OF WORK DONE	MILEAGE	LOCATION/ COMPANY	REPLACEMENT PARTS (if applicable)	COST

License Plate No: _____ **VEHICLE MAINTENANCE LOG BOOK** Make/Model/Year: _____

DATE	DESCRIPTION OF WORK DONE	MILEAGE	LOCATION/ COMPANY	REPLACEMENT PARTS (if applicable)	COST

License Plate No: _____   **VEHICLE MAINTENANCE LOG BOOK**   **Make/Model/Year:** _____

DATE	DESCRIPTION OF WORK DONE	MILEAGE	LOCATION/ COMPANY	REPLACEMENT PARTS *(if applicable)*	COST

License Plate No: _____ **VEHICLE MAINTENANCE LOG BOOK** Make/Model/Year: _____

DATE	DESCRIPTION OF WORK DONE	MILEAGE	LOCATION/ COMPANY	REPLACEMENT PARTS *(if applicable)*	COST

License Plate No: _____ **VEHICLE MAINTENANCE LOG BOOK** **Make/Model/Year:** _____

DATE	DESCRIPTION OF WORK DONE	MILEAGE	LOCATION/ COMPANY	REPLACEMENT PARTS *(if applicable)*	COST

License Plate No: _____ **VEHICLE MAINTENANCE LOG BOOK** **Make/Model/Year:** _____

DATE	DESCRIPTION OF WORK DONE	MILEAGE	LOCATION/ COMPANY	REPLACEMENT PARTS *(if applicable)*	COST

License Plate No: _____   **VEHICLE MAINTENANCE LOG BOOK**   **Make/Model/Year:** _____

DATE	DESCRIPTION OF WORK DONE	MILEAGE	LOCATION/ COMPANY	REPLACEMENT PARTS *(if applicable)*	COST

License Plate No: _____ **VEHICLE MAINTENANCE LOG BOOK** Make/Model/Year: _____

DATE	DESCRIPTION OF WORK DONE	MILEAGE	LOCATION/ COMPANY	REPLACEMENT PARTS *(if applicable)*	COST

License Plate No: _____ **VEHICLE MAINTENANCE LOG BOOK** Make/Model/Year: _____

DATE	DESCRIPTION OF WORK DONE	MILEAGE	LOCATION/ COMPANY	REPLACEMENT PARTS *(if applicable)*	COST

License Plate No: _____   **VEHICLE MAINTENANCE LOG BOOK**   **Make/Model/Year:** _____

DATE	DESCRIPTION OF WORK DONE	MILEAGE	LOCATION/ COMPANY	REPLACEMENT PARTS *(if applicable)*	COST

License Plate No: _____   **VEHICLE MAINTENANCE LOG BOOK**   **Make/Model/Year:** _____

DATE	DESCRIPTION OF WORK DONE	MILEAGE	LOCATION/ COMPANY	REPLACEMENT PARTS *(if applicable)*	COST

License Plate No: _____   **VEHICLE MAINTENANCE LOG BOOK**   **Make/Model/Year:** _____

DATE	DESCRIPTION OF WORK DONE	MILEAGE	LOCATION/ COMPANY	REPLACEMENT PARTS (if applicable)	COST

License Plate No: _____ **VEHICLE MAINTENANCE LOG BOOK** **Make/Model/Year:** _____

DATE	DESCRIPTION OF WORK DONE	MILEAGE	LOCATION/ COMPANY	REPLACEMENT PARTS *(if applicable)*	COST

License Plate No: _____ **VEHICLE MAINTENANCE LOG BOOK** **Make/Model/Year:** _____

DATE	DESCRIPTION OF WORK DONE	MILEAGE	LOCATION/ COMPANY	REPLACEMENT PARTS (if applicable)	COST

License Plate No: _____ **VEHICLE MAINTENANCE LOG BOOK** Make/Model/Year: _____

DATE	DESCRIPTION OF WORK DONE	MILEAGE	LOCATION/ COMPANY	REPLACEMENT PARTS *(if applicable)*	COST

License Plate No: _____   **VEHICLE MAINTENANCE LOG BOOK**   **Make/Model/Year:** _____

DATE	DESCRIPTION OF WORK DONE	MILEAGE	LOCATION/ COMPANY	REPLACEMENT PARTS (if applicable)	COST

License Plate No: _____ **VEHICLE MAINTENANCE LOG BOOK** Make/Model/Year: _____

DATE	DESCRIPTION OF WORK DONE	MILEAGE	LOCATION/ COMPANY	REPLACEMENT PARTS (if applicable)	COST

License Plate No: _____ **VEHICLE MAINTENANCE LOG BOOK** Make/Model/Year: _____

DATE	DESCRIPTION OF WORK DONE	MILEAGE	LOCATION/ COMPANY	REPLACEMENT PARTS *(if applicable)*	COST

License Plate No: _____ **VEHICLE MAINTENANCE LOG BOOK** **Make/Model/Year:** _____

DATE	DESCRIPTION OF WORK DONE	MILEAGE	LOCATION/ COMPANY	REPLACEMENT PARTS *(if applicable)*	COST

License Plate No: _____ **VEHICLE MAINTENANCE LOG BOOK** Make/Model/Year: _____

DATE	DESCRIPTION OF WORK DONE	MILEAGE	LOCATION/ COMPANY	REPLACEMENT PARTS *(if applicable)*	COST

License Plate No: _____   **VEHICLE MAINTENANCE LOG BOOK**   **Make/Model/Year:** _____

DATE	DESCRIPTION OF WORK DONE	MILEAGE	LOCATION/ COMPANY	REPLACEMENT PARTS (if applicable)	COST

License Plate No: _____   **VEHICLE MAINTENANCE LOG BOOK**   **Make/Model/Year:** _____

DATE	DESCRIPTION OF WORK DONE	MILEAGE	LOCATION/ COMPANY	REPLACEMENT PARTS *(if applicable)*	COST

License Plate No: _____ **VEHICLE MAINTENANCE LOG BOOK** **Make/Model/Year:** _____

DATE	DESCRIPTION OF WORK DONE	MILEAGE	LOCATION/ COMPANY	REPLACEMENT PARTS *(if applicable)*	COST

License Plate No: _____   **VEHICLE MAINTENANCE LOG BOOK**   Make/Model/Year: _____

DATE	DESCRIPTION OF WORK DONE	MILEAGE	LOCATION/ COMPANY	REPLACEMENT PARTS *(if applicable)*	COST

License Plate No: _____ **VEHICLE MAINTENANCE LOG BOOK** **Make/Model/Year:** _____

DATE	DESCRIPTION OF WORK DONE	MILEAGE	LOCATION/ COMPANY	REPLACEMENT PARTS (if applicable)	COST

License Plate No: _____ **VEHICLE MAINTENANCE LOG BOOK** Make/Model/Year: _____

DATE	DESCRIPTION OF WORK DONE	MILEAGE	LOCATION/ COMPANY	REPLACEMENT PARTS *(if applicable)*	COST

License Plate No: _____ **VEHICLE MAINTENANCE LOG BOOK** Make/Model/Year: _____

DATE	DESCRIPTION OF WORK DONE	MILEAGE	LOCATION/ COMPANY	REPLACEMENT PARTS *(if applicable)*	COST

License Plate No: _____   **VEHICLE MAINTENANCE LOG BOOK**   **Make/Model/Year:** _____

DATE	DESCRIPTION OF WORK DONE	MILEAGE	LOCATION/ COMPANY	REPLACEMENT PARTS *(if applicable)*	COST

License Plate No: _____ **VEHICLE MAINTENANCE LOG BOOK** Make/Model/Year: _____

DATE	DESCRIPTION OF WORK DONE	MILEAGE	LOCATION/ COMPANY	REPLACEMENT PARTS *(if applicable)*	COST

License Plate No: _____   **VEHICLE MAINTENANCE LOG BOOK**   Make/Model/Year: _____

DATE	DESCRIPTION OF WORK DONE	MILEAGE	LOCATION/ COMPANY	REPLACEMENT PARTS *(if applicable)*	COST

License Plate No: _____ **VEHICLE MAINTENANCE LOG BOOK** Make/Model/Year: _____

DATE	DESCRIPTION OF WORK DONE	MILEAGE	LOCATION/ COMPANY	REPLACEMENT PARTS *(if applicable)*	COST

License Plate No: _____   **VEHICLE MAINTENANCE LOG BOOK**   Make/Model/Year: _____

DATE	DESCRIPTION OF WORK DONE	MILEAGE	LOCATION/ COMPANY	REPLACEMENT PARTS (if applicable)	COST

License Plate No: _____ **VEHICLE MAINTENANCE LOG BOOK** **Make/Model/Year:** _____

DATE	DESCRIPTION OF WORK DONE	MILEAGE	LOCATION/ COMPANY	REPLACEMENT PARTS *(if applicable)*	COST

License Plate No: _____ **VEHICLE MAINTENANCE LOG BOOK** Make/Model/Year: _____

DATE	DESCRIPTION OF WORK DONE	MILEAGE	LOCATION/ COMPANY	REPLACEMENT PARTS *(if applicable)*	COST

License Plate No: _____ **VEHICLE MAINTENANCE LOG BOOK** **Make/Model/Year:** _____

DATE	DESCRIPTION OF WORK DONE	MILEAGE	LOCATION/ COMPANY	REPLACEMENT PARTS *(if applicable)*	COST

License Plate No: _____   **VEHICLE MAINTENANCE LOG BOOK**   Make/Model/Year: _____

DATE	DESCRIPTION OF WORK DONE	MILEAGE	LOCATION/ COMPANY	REPLACEMENT PARTS *(if applicable)*	COST

License Plate No: _____ **VEHICLE MAINTENANCE LOG BOOK** Make/Model/Year: _____

DATE	DESCRIPTION OF WORK DONE	MILEAGE	LOCATION/ COMPANY	REPLACEMENT PARTS (if applicable)	COST

License Plate No: _____   **VEHICLE MAINTENANCE LOG BOOK**   Make/Model/Year: _____

DATE	DESCRIPTION OF WORK DONE	MILEAGE	LOCATION/ COMPANY	REPLACEMENT PARTS *(if applicable)*	COST

License Plate No: _____   **VEHICLE MAINTENANCE LOG BOOK**   **Make/Model/Year:** _____

DATE	DESCRIPTION OF WORK DONE	MILEAGE	LOCATION/ COMPANY	REPLACEMENT PARTS *(if applicable)*	COST

License Plate No: _____ **VEHICLE MAINTENANCE LOG BOOK** **Make/Model/Year:** _____

DATE	DESCRIPTION OF WORK DONE	MILEAGE	LOCATION/ COMPANY	REPLACEMENT PARTS *(if applicable)*	COST

License Plate No: _____   **VEHICLE MAINTENANCE LOG BOOK**   **Make/Model/Year:** _____

DATE	DESCRIPTION OF WORK DONE	MILEAGE	LOCATION/ COMPANY	REPLACEMENT PARTS *(if applicable)*	COST

License Plate No: _____   **VEHICLE MAINTENANCE LOG BOOK**   Make/Model/Year: _____

DATE	DESCRIPTION OF WORK DONE	MILEAGE	LOCATION/ COMPANY	REPLACEMENT PARTS *(if applicable)*	COST

License Plate No: _____ **VEHICLE MAINTENANCE LOG BOOK** **Make/Model/Year:** _____

DATE	DESCRIPTION OF WORK DONE	MILEAGE	LOCATION/ COMPANY	REPLACEMENT PARTS *(if applicable)*	COST

License Plate No: _____ **VEHICLE MAINTENANCE LOG BOOK** **Make/Model/Year:** _____

DATE	DESCRIPTION OF WORK DONE	MILEAGE	LOCATION/ COMPANY	REPLACEMENT PARTS *(if applicable)*	COST

License Plate No: _____   **VEHICLE MAINTENANCE LOG BOOK**   **Make/Model/Year:** _____

DATE	DESCRIPTION OF WORK DONE	MILEAGE	LOCATION/ COMPANY	REPLACEMENT PARTS *(if applicable)*	COST

License Plate No: _____ **VEHICLE MAINTENANCE LOG BOOK** **Make/Model/Year:** _____

DATE	DESCRIPTION OF WORK DONE	MILEAGE	LOCATION/ COMPANY	REPLACEMENT PARTS *(if applicable)*	COST

License Plate No: _____ **VEHICLE MAINTENANCE LOG BOOK** **Make/Model/Year:** _____

DATE	DESCRIPTION OF WORK DONE	MILEAGE	LOCATION/ COMPANY	REPLACEMENT PARTS *(if applicable)*	COST

License Plate No: _____   **VEHICLE MAINTENANCE LOG BOOK**   Make/Model/Year: _____

DATE	DESCRIPTION OF WORK DONE	MILEAGE	LOCATION/ COMPANY	REPLACEMENT PARTS *(if applicable)*	COST

License Plate No: _____   **VEHICLE MAINTENANCE LOG BOOK**   **Make/Model/Year:** _____

DATE	DESCRIPTION OF WORK DONE	MILEAGE	LOCATION/ COMPANY	REPLACEMENT PARTS (if applicable)	COST

License Plate No: _____   **VEHICLE MAINTENANCE LOG BOOK**   Make/Model/Year: _____

DATE	DESCRIPTION OF WORK DONE	MILEAGE	LOCATION/ COMPANY	REPLACEMENT PARTS *(if applicable)*	COST

License Plate No: _____ **VEHICLE MAINTENANCE LOG BOOK** **Make/Model/Year:** _____

DATE	DESCRIPTION OF WORK DONE	MILEAGE	LOCATION/ COMPANY	REPLACEMENT PARTS (if applicable)	COST

License Plate No: _____ **VEHICLE MAINTENANCE LOG BOOK** **Make/Model/Year:** _____

DATE	DESCRIPTION OF WORK DONE	MILEAGE	LOCATION/ COMPANY	REPLACEMENT PARTS *(if applicable)*	COST

License Plate No: _____   **VEHICLE MAINTENANCE LOG BOOK**   **Make/Model/Year:** _____

DATE	DESCRIPTION OF WORK DONE	MILEAGE	LOCATION/ COMPANY	REPLACEMENT PARTS (if applicable)	COST

License Plate No: _____   **VEHICLE MAINTENANCE LOG BOOK**   Make/Model/Year: _____

DATE	DESCRIPTION OF WORK DONE	MILEAGE	LOCATION/ COMPANY	REPLACEMENT PARTS *(if applicable)*	COST

License Plate No: _____ **VEHICLE MAINTENANCE LOG BOOK** **Make/Model/Year:** _____

DATE	DESCRIPTION OF WORK DONE	MILEAGE	LOCATION/ COMPANY	REPLACEMENT PARTS *(if applicable)*	COST

License Plate No: _____   **VEHICLE MAINTENANCE LOG BOOK**   Make/Model/Year: _____

DATE	DESCRIPTION OF WORK DONE	MILEAGE	LOCATION/ COMPANY	REPLACEMENT PARTS *(if applicable)*	COST

License Plate No: _____ **VEHICLE MAINTENANCE LOG BOOK** Make/Model/Year: _____

DATE	DESCRIPTION OF WORK DONE	MILEAGE	LOCATION/ COMPANY	REPLACEMENT PARTS (if applicable)	COST

License Plate No: _____   **VEHICLE MAINTENANCE LOG BOOK**   **Make/Model/Year:** _____

DATE	DESCRIPTION OF WORK DONE	MILEAGE	LOCATION/ COMPANY	REPLACEMENT PARTS *(if applicable)*	COST

License Plate No: _____ **VEHICLE MAINTENANCE LOG BOOK** **Make/Model/Year:** _____

DATE	DESCRIPTION OF WORK DONE	MILEAGE	LOCATION/ COMPANY	REPLACEMENT PARTS *(if applicable)*	COST

License Plate No: _____ **VEHICLE MAINTENANCE LOG BOOK** **Make/Model/Year:** _____

DATE	DESCRIPTION OF WORK DONE	MILEAGE	LOCATION/ COMPANY	REPLACEMENT PARTS (if applicable)	COST

License Plate No: _____   **VEHICLE MAINTENANCE LOG BOOK**   **Make/Model/Year:** _____

DATE	DESCRIPTION OF WORK DONE	MILEAGE	LOCATION/ COMPANY	REPLACEMENT PARTS *(if applicable)*	COST

License Plate No: _____   **VEHICLE MAINTENANCE LOG BOOK**   **Make/Model/Year:** _____

DATE	DESCRIPTION OF WORK DONE	MILEAGE	LOCATION/ COMPANY	REPLACEMENT PARTS *(if applicable)*	COST

License Plate No: _____ **VEHICLE MAINTENANCE LOG BOOK** **Make/Model/Year:** _____

DATE	DESCRIPTION OF WORK DONE	MILEAGE	LOCATION/ COMPANY	REPLACEMENT PARTS *(if applicable)*	COST

License Plate No: _____   **VEHICLE MAINTENANCE LOG BOOK**   Make/Model/Year: _____

DATE	DESCRIPTION OF WORK DONE	MILEAGE	LOCATION/ COMPANY	REPLACEMENT PARTS *(if applicable)*	COST

License Plate No: _____   **VEHICLE MAINTENANCE LOG BOOK**   Make/Model/Year: _____

DATE	DESCRIPTION OF WORK DONE	MILEAGE	LOCATION/ COMPANY	REPLACEMENT PARTS *(if applicable)*	COST

License Plate No: _____   **VEHICLE MAINTENANCE LOG BOOK**   **Make/Model/Year:** _____

DATE	DESCRIPTION OF WORK DONE	MILEAGE	LOCATION/ COMPANY	REPLACEMENT PARTS *(if applicable)*	COST

License Plate No: _____ **VEHICLE MAINTENANCE LOG BOOK** Make/Model/Year: _____

DATE	DESCRIPTION OF WORK DONE	MILEAGE	LOCATION/ COMPANY	REPLACEMENT PARTS *(if applicable)*	COST

License Plate No: _____   **VEHICLE MAINTENANCE LOG BOOK**   Make/Model/Year: _____

DATE	DESCRIPTION OF WORK DONE	MILEAGE	LOCATION/ COMPANY	REPLACEMENT PARTS (if applicable)	COST

License Plate No: _____ **VEHICLE MAINTENANCE LOG BOOK** Make/Model/Year: _____

DATE	DESCRIPTION OF WORK DONE	MILEAGE	LOCATION/ COMPANY	REPLACEMENT PARTS *(if applicable)*	COST

License Plate No: _____ **VEHICLE MAINTENANCE LOG BOOK** Make/Model/Year: _____

DATE	DESCRIPTION OF WORK DONE	MILEAGE	LOCATION/ COMPANY	REPLACEMENT PARTS *(if applicable)*	COST

License Plate No: _____ **VEHICLE MAINTENANCE LOG BOOK** **Make/Model/Year:** _____

DATE	DESCRIPTION OF WORK DONE	MILEAGE	LOCATION/ COMPANY	REPLACEMENT PARTS *(if applicable)*	COST

License Plate No: _____   **VEHICLE MAINTENANCE LOG BOOK**   **Make/Model/Year:** _____

DATE	DESCRIPTION OF WORK DONE	MILEAGE	LOCATION/ COMPANY	REPLACEMENT PARTS *(if applicable)*	COST

License Plate No: _____   **VEHICLE MAINTENANCE LOG BOOK**   Make/Model/Year: _____

DATE	DESCRIPTION OF WORK DONE	MILEAGE	LOCATION/ COMPANY	REPLACEMENT PARTS (if applicable)	COST

License Plate No: _____   **VEHICLE MAINTENANCE LOG BOOK**   **Make/Model/Year:** _____

DATE	DESCRIPTION OF WORK DONE	MILEAGE	LOCATION/ COMPANY	REPLACEMENT PARTS *(if applicable)*	COST

License Plate No: _____   **VEHICLE MAINTENANCE LOG BOOK**   **Make/Model/Year:** _____

DATE	DESCRIPTION OF WORK DONE	MILEAGE	LOCATION/ COMPANY	REPLACEMENT PARTS *(if applicable)*	COST

License Plate No: _____ **VEHICLE MAINTENANCE LOG BOOK** **Make/Model/Year:** _____

DATE	DESCRIPTION OF WORK DONE	MILEAGE	LOCATION/ COMPANY	REPLACEMENT PARTS *(if applicable)*	COST

License Plate No: _____   **VEHICLE MAINTENANCE LOG BOOK**   **Make/Model/Year:** _____

DATE	DESCRIPTION OF WORK DONE	MILEAGE	LOCATION/ COMPANY	REPLACEMENT PARTS *(if applicable)*	COST

License Plate No: _____ **VEHICLE MAINTENANCE LOG BOOK** **Make/Model/Year:** _____

DATE	DESCRIPTION OF WORK DONE	MILEAGE	LOCATION/ COMPANY	REPLACEMENT PARTS *(if applicable)*	COST

License Plate No: _____   **VEHICLE MAINTENANCE LOG BOOK**   **Make/Model/Year:** _____

DATE	DESCRIPTION OF WORK DONE	MILEAGE	LOCATION/ COMPANY	REPLACEMENT PARTS *(if applicable)*	COST

License Plate No: _____ **VEHICLE MAINTENANCE LOG BOOK** **Make/Model/Year:** _____

DATE	DESCRIPTION OF WORK DONE	MILEAGE	LOCATION/ COMPANY	REPLACEMENT PARTS *(if applicable)*	COST

License Plate No: _____   **VEHICLE MAINTENANCE LOG BOOK**   **Make/Model/Year:** _____

DATE	DESCRIPTION OF WORK DONE	MILEAGE	LOCATION/ COMPANY	REPLACEMENT PARTS *(if applicable)*	COST

License Plate No: _____   **VEHICLE MAINTENANCE LOG BOOK**   Make/Model/Year: _____

DATE	DESCRIPTION OF WORK DONE	MILEAGE	LOCATION/ COMPANY	REPLACEMENT PARTS (if applicable)	COST

License Plate No: _____ **VEHICLE MAINTENANCE LOG BOOK** Make/Model/Year: _____

DATE	DESCRIPTION OF WORK DONE	MILEAGE	LOCATION/ COMPANY	REPLACEMENT PARTS (if applicable)	COST

License Plate No: _____   **VEHICLE MAINTENANCE LOG BOOK**   **Make/Model/Year:** _____

DATE	DESCRIPTION OF WORK DONE	MILEAGE	LOCATION/ COMPANY	REPLACEMENT PARTS *(if applicable)*	COST

License Plate No: _____ **VEHICLE MAINTENANCE LOG BOOK** **Make/Model/Year:** _____

DATE	DESCRIPTION OF WORK DONE	MILEAGE	LOCATION/ COMPANY	REPLACEMENT PARTS *(if applicable)*	COST

License Plate No: _____   **VEHICLE MAINTENANCE LOG BOOK**   **Make/Model/Year:** _____

DATE	DESCRIPTION OF WORK DONE	MILEAGE	LOCATION/ COMPANY	REPLACEMENT PARTS *(if applicable)*	COST

License Plate No: _____ **VEHICLE MAINTENANCE LOG BOOK** Make/Model/Year: _____

DATE	DESCRIPTION OF WORK DONE	MILEAGE	LOCATION/ COMPANY	REPLACEMENT PARTS (if applicable)	COST

License Plate No: _____ **VEHICLE MAINTENANCE LOG BOOK** Make/Model/Year: _____

DATE	DESCRIPTION OF WORK DONE	MILEAGE	LOCATION/ COMPANY	REPLACEMENT PARTS *(if applicable)*	COST

License Plate No: _____   **VEHICLE MAINTENANCE LOG BOOK**   **Make/Model/Year:** _____

DATE	DESCRIPTION OF WORK DONE	MILEAGE	LOCATION/ COMPANY	REPLACEMENT PARTS (if applicable)	COST

License Plate No: _____ **VEHICLE MAINTENANCE LOG BOOK** **Make/Model/Year:** _____

DATE	DESCRIPTION OF WORK DONE	MILEAGE	LOCATION/ COMPANY	REPLACEMENT PARTS *(if applicable)*	COST

License Plate No: _____   **VEHICLE MAINTENANCE LOG BOOK**   **Make/Model/Year:** _____

DATE	DESCRIPTION OF WORK DONE	MILEAGE	LOCATION/ COMPANY	REPLACEMENT PARTS *(if applicable)*	COST

License Plate No: _____ **VEHICLE MAINTENANCE LOG BOOK** Make/Model/Year: _____

DATE	DESCRIPTION OF WORK DONE	MILEAGE	LOCATION/ COMPANY	REPLACEMENT PARTS *(if applicable)*	COST

License Plate No: _____   **VEHICLE MAINTENANCE LOG BOOK**   **Make/Model/Year:** _____

DATE	DESCRIPTION OF WORK DONE	MILEAGE	LOCATION/ COMPANY	REPLACEMENT PARTS (if applicable)	COST

License Plate No: _____ **VEHICLE MAINTENANCE LOG BOOK** Make/Model/Year: _____

DATE	DESCRIPTION OF WORK DONE	MILEAGE	LOCATION/ COMPANY	REPLACEMENT PARTS (if applicable)	COST

License Plate No: _____ **VEHICLE MAINTENANCE LOG BOOK** Make/Model/Year: _____

DATE	DESCRIPTION OF WORK DONE	MILEAGE	LOCATION/ COMPANY	REPLACEMENT PARTS *(if applicable)*	COST

Made in the USA
Middletown, DE
17 January 2022